For Matt and Rach, Charlie and Abby. CS

For Mus and Rory. JR

First published by Allen & Unwin in 2026

Allen & Unwin
Cammeraygal Country
83 Alexander Street
Crows Nest NSW 2065
Australia
Phone: (61 2) 8425 0100
Email: info@allenandunwin.com
Web: www.allenandunwin.com

*Allen & Unwin acknowledges the Traditional Owners of the Country on which we live and work.
We pay our respects to all Aboriginal and Torres Strait Islander Elders, past and present.*

EU Authorised Representative: Easy Access System Europe, Mustamäe tee 50,
10621 Tallinn, Estonia, gpsr.requests@easproject.com

A catalogue record for this book is available from the National Library of Australia

ISBN 978 1 76118 171 9

For teaching resources, explore allenandunwin.com/learn

Illustration technique: watercolour, acrylic painting, collage, pencil, ink and digital illustration

Cover and text design by Sandra Nobes
Set in 18 pt CenturyOS MT Std, with hand lettering by Jess Racklyeft
This book was printed in November 2025 by C&C Offset Printing Co. Ltd, China

1 3 5 7 9 10 8 6 4 2

www.clairesaxby.com
www.jessesmess.com

Claire Saxby • Jess Racklyeft

On a summer beach, a pair of plovers prepare a nest. Waiting.

Above the glassy sea, an eagle hovers. Watching.

Beneath the surface, a spiky green fish sways. Waiting.

Periwinkle tracks scribble across
a blister rock pool to where edge-tucked
anemones extend tentacles wide.
A crab scuttles. Watching.
A storm is rising.

It begins with a puff. Then another.

A flutter, a ripple, a shiver show where it blows.

Cotton ball clouds appear overhead.

The breeze builds. Clouds grow.

The plovers retreat into the dunes.
The eagle rides the rising wind up the escarpment
and beyond, to her sheltered nest.
Rock pool anemones close. The crab tucks tight.
Periwinkles cling to rock walls.
White-lipped waves snack at the shore.
Sand flurries. Clouds cluster.

Inside the cloud, updrafts race by downdrafts.
Tiny water drops join and grow
until they are too heavy to stay aloft.
Sparks flash and grumble.
The storm is here.

On the reef, the green fish retreats.

A star drops from seagrass, edges closer to others.

Everything echoes the breath from the sea.

Back, forth. Back-forth.

Lightning cracks and thunder bellows.
Fat raindrops plit and plop.
The wind is alive.
It flings and slings rain at the land, at the sea.

The storm rips kelp from the reef and hurls it at the shore.
Shredded seagrass turns the froth green
as lightning flashes and thunder roars.
Waves gouge the shore now
as wind shatters the tidal wrack line.

Rain spears the water, craters the sand.
The reef disappears in a tumult
of wind-built bubbles and wave churn.
The rock pool blows empty, then refills with sand-wash.

And then – just like that – the storm ends.

The beach is cool now, as cool as the air.
Waves gentle.
Froth bubbles pop.
The wind falls away and everything stills
in the storm-thrashed bay.

The spiky green fish emerges to nibble at sea lettuce.
Anemones bloom. Periwinkles lay new tracks.
The eagle soars over the escarpment. Watching.
The plover pair emerge from the dunes
onto a clear-sky sunset beach, to build a new nest.
Waiting.

We can't see wind, but we can see what it does. We can feel it, too. When summer sands are hotter than the water that laps the shore, the hot air rises and cooler air moves in from the sea, creating a breeze. Sometimes this air movement can cause a storm. Increased global temperatures and rising sea levels heighten the chance of more severe, more damaging thunderstorms.